Original title:
Scarves and Serendipity

Copyright © 2025 Creative Arts Management OÜ
All rights reserved.

Author: Simon Fairchild
ISBN HARDBACK: 978-1-80586-074-7
ISBN PAPERBACK: 978-1-80586-546-9

The Hidden Patterns of Happening

In a cupboard filled with fluff,
I found a twist of luck, not tough.
It danced like socks on laundry day,
While the cat just watched in dismay.

A tumble here, a shuffle there,
Patterns giggle in the air.
Mismatched gloves come out to play,
In a waltz that brightens gray.

Serene Twists of Fate

Some say fate wears goofy hats,
They vibrate like a bunch of bats.
Stumbling through a waiting line,
I grabbed a donut, felt divine.

Eager serendipity sings,
As fortune flaps its silly wings.
A hiccup here, a laugh, a cheer,
Unexpected joy draws near.

Woven Whispers of Chance

Once found a thread in a stew,
A strange connection, who knew?
Whispers tangled in the night,
Turned an evening into delight.

A puppet's dance, a pisces leap,
While giggling friends refuse to sleep.
We stitch together laughter's seam,
In a tapestry of each dream.

Threads of Unexpected Journeys

On a bus with a dancing mole,
I found a foot with quite a role.
It tapped and twirled, a funny sight,
As passengers giggled in delight.

A ride to nowhere led us here,
Where jellybeans appeared in cheer.
Through silly maps and jumbled ties,
We weave our tales, with joyful sighs.

Whispers of the Unexpected Journey

A twist of fate, oh what a day,
A tangled knot led me astray.
I tripped on a length of bright maroon,
And danced like a fool to a silly tune.

Strangers laughed, they pointed and cheered,
My fashion faux pas, it clearly appeared.
Yet in the chaos, I found a delight,
Unexpected smiles lit up the night.

Magic Woven in a Silk Embrace

In a café, my drink took a dive,
My charming scarf? It soon came alive!
Swirling around like a playful breeze,
It danced on the table, oh what a tease!

It snagged a croissant, fluttered with glee,
With each little rip, I knew I was free.
A patisserie's laughter rang through the air,
As crumbs met fabric in a whimsical pair.

Unexpected Journeys in Wool and Thread

A ball of yarn rolled down the street,
I chased it fast on my silly feet.
Like a puppy lost in a thrilling chase,
To make a new friend? What a great place!

I found a cat who enjoyed the thrill,
Pouncing at colors, with time to kill.
Two odd companions, threading along,
Creating a tale that felt like a song.

The Colors of Happy Happenstance

A rainbow fell on my outstretched arm,
As I twirled around without any harm.
A splash of yellow met a hint of blue,
And dance partners joined in, multicolored too!

Laughter erupted, the world felt right,
In a garden of happenstance, pure delight.
We twirled 'til dusk, all shades seemed to flirt,
With joy in our hearts and paint on our shirt.

The Art of the Unexpected Stitch

In the corner of a drawer, a thread unwinds,
A misfit patch takes shape, surprising minds.
With laughter bubbling up, we stitch together,
A tale of knots and twists, light as a feather.

The needle dances wildly, a faux pas parade,
Tangled yarns and mismatched hues, a charade.
We chuckle at the patterns, oh what a sight,
In this fashion frenzy, chaos feels just right.

Moments Wrapped in Warmth

A colorful scene where the silly threads play,
An old creation whispers, 'I'm here for the day!'
With a playful wink, it swirled around me,
Turning chill into joy; oh, what can it be?

We huddle close, sipping cocoa so sweet,
Wrapped in our layers, tangled feet.
Life's comical moments, like yarn, they entwine,
Creating a quilt, warm from the divine.

Chance Encounters against a Knitted Sky

Under a knitted blanket, clouds loom above,
A shy thread of fate gives a nudge of love.
Two strangers collide in a colorful mash,
Their laughter ignites, leaving a splash!

Fates interwoven, like threads in a loom,
As colors collide, dispelling all gloom.
Oh, the serendipity of tangled delight,
In the fabric of fortune, we dance through the night.

Weathered Fabrics and New Beginnings

A patch on my elbow tells tales of the past,
Worn and weathered, yet made to last.
With every frayed edge, stories emerge,
Of bizarre adventures, each stitch a surge.

So bring on the mishaps, and the laughter they yield,
Every bump in the fabric is better revealed.
Because in every twist, there's humor to find,
In the art of creation, we leave doubts behind.

Tapestries of Happy Accidents

Threads of fate weave with glee,
A tangled mess, oh what a spree!
Laughter erupts in colorful swirls,
As knots become gifts in this fabric world.

Dropping stitches, a stitch in time,
Each twist of yarn, a silly rhyme.
Bumbled weavers find their groove,
In a patchwork dance, we all can move.

The Veil of Hidden Possibilities

A wink from fate behind the folds,
Jokes that glimmer like tales of old.
What lies beneath this fabric guise?
Unexpected chuckles, a sweet surprise.

Whirling around in a pastel blur,
A fashion show, just wait, confer!
With each layer, laughter peeks,
In whispered threads, the heart just squeaks.

Lush Layers of Fortunate Encounters

Beneath bright layers, joy does bloom,
With every twist, dispel the gloom.
Draped in warmth, friendships ignite,
As laughter dances through the night.

Each wrap a tale, surprising and grand,
Stumbling moments become well-planned.
Bumbling beauty, oh what a sight,
In cozy folds, we take flight.

Unexpected Twists in Cozy Wraps

In cozy folds where secrets lie,
A twist of fate; oh my, oh my!
The fabric flows, a comical spree,
Bumbling styles, just wait and see.

With every turn, a chuckle here,
Wrapped in warmth, we cast off fear.
Funky patterns zigzag and laugh,
In each embrace, we find our path.

Embracing the Unexpected Stitches

A tangled yarn in a playful mess,
Knots and loops, oh what a dress!
Colors clash in a wild dance,
Who knew wool could lead to romance?

A bright blue thread on a polka dot,
It suits my look—well, maybe not!
Yet laughter rolls like a ball of fluff,
Wearing crazy makes life less tough.

Touched by Chance's Gentle Hand

A splash of green, oh what a sight,
In the laundry basket, it took flight.
A sock that vanished, what a thrill,
Now I'm left with a one-legged chill.

The dryer mouths my vibrant sins,
Where did you go? I need your twins!
But here I stand in mismatched flair,
Who knew laundry could spark such hair?

Threads of Fate in a Winding Path

On the street, I march with glee,
Wearing stripes, oh can't you see?
A twist of fate, a mishap bright,
Threading chaos into delight.

Patterned socks, a joyful quilt,
Fashion faux pas that I have built.
Yet every glance brings a grin or two,
Life's best moments are silly and blue.

Joyful Patterns of the Unforeseen

In a market, a fabric called fate,
I tripped and tumbled, oh isn't it great?
With a scarf that flaged like a pirate's hat,
I danced past the stall with a graceful splat.

A twist of fabric around my neck,
Makes quite the statement, what the heck!
Sometimes style comes from a joyful fall,
And laughter stitches the best of all.

Secrets Woven into Every Fiber

In a cupboard, colors hide,
An orange twirl, a purple slide.
Who knew that knots could bring such glee?
With laughter loud, it's hard to see.

A fuzzy yarn so out of place,
Tickled pink, I joined the race.
Twisting tales with every turn,
Oh, what fun, I still can learn!

Solace in the Stitching of Fate

Threaded moments, a snug embrace,
Each stitch whispers, 'Join the chase!'
A crumpled ball and tangled spree,
What joy, oh dear, come join me free!

Purls and pearls in mismatched glow,
A tangled dance, we steal the show.
With each loop, another laugh,
Time ticks fast, take our photograph!

Musings in a Tangle of Threads

Chasing whims where colors blend,
A playful chase, around the bend.
Fingers flying, oh what a sight,
Stitching joy both day and night!

A rogue knot just won't let go,
Embarrassment? Nah, just a show!
We'll twirl and twist till morning light,
Each misstep feels just so right!

A Festival of Happy Accidents

A ball of fluff, I trip and roll,
With unplanned flair, I weave my soul.
Who knew a slip could spark such cheer?
With giggles shared, the end is near!

Loops and swirls, a crazy maze,
Found the joy amidst the blaze.
What started as a tangled trail,
Now dances in our hearty hail!

Whispers of Woven Threads

In a tangled mess, threads collide,
A yarn that wraps, but won't abide.
Laughter twirls in every fold,
A story stitched, fun to be told.

Granny's gift, a treasure rare,
It tickles noses, gives quite a scare.
Wrapped around, we dance and spin,
A fashion choice? You lose or win.

Patterns clash in vivid display,
As we trip and giggle on our way.
Who knew that warmth could lead to this?
A cozy hug, with a side of bliss.

Chance Encounters in the Silk Mist

Through the fog of silken dreams,
Hilarity hides in whimsical seams.
Bumped and tangled, we both fall,
Laughing loud, with no care at all.

Your hat's askew, my shoe's unwound,
Life's best moments are often found.
In chance meetings, mischief sparks,
Creating joy, igniting darks.

Fates entwined like playful vines,
We swap our quirks, and share the signs.
Oh, what a jolly crowded scene,
In a world that's whimsically keen!

The Knotted Embrace

Knot this, knot that, what a mess!
Underneath, we laugh and guess.
A twist of fate, a loop of cheer,
In every tangle, friends draw near.

Hilarious mishaps, who knew we'd grin?
A braided bond where laughter begins.
Tangled tales of joy and jest,
In knotted embrace, we find the best.

Colors of Fortune

Dancing hues in splendid flare,
They swirl around, without a care.
Stitch by stitch, we paint the day,
Brighter and bolder, in disarray.

A palette rich with giggles shared,
Jests and jabs, nobody's scared.
Every color tells a tale,
In this wild ride, we shall not fail.

A Journey in Every Loop

A twist of fate in every thread,
You'll find new paths where you're led.
Like tangled yarn upon the floor,
Each loop reveals an opened door.

The world unfolds in every weave,
You might get lost, but don't you grieve.
For every twist, there's laughter near,
Embrace the chaos, never fear.

With colors bright, and patterns wild,
Each twist and turn, a curious child.
In every knot, a silly tale,
Adventure calls like a playful gale.

The Art of Unexpected Discovery

In pockets deep, odd treasures hide,
A sock with stripes or keys that slide.
Life throws surprises all about,
With curious finds, there's no doubt.

Fuzzy friends that dance and play,
You never know what's here to stay.
A missing glove, a hat askew,
Make for mishaps, oh so true!

While searching high and looking low,
You stumble on a funny show.
With each new twist, a twist of fate,
Forget the clock, let's celebrate!

Cascade of Colors

Colors clash in cheerful glee,
A rainbow bursting wild and free.
Each hue a giggle, each shade a chime,
Dancing together, oh so sublime.

Turn your back, and watch it fly,
A pink and green that caught your eye.
While tripping on this vibrant spree,
Mayhem bloomed in jubilee.

A splash of orange, a splash of blue,
Bring smiles and hugs, this much is true.
In every fiber, joy will seep,
Dive on in, and take a leap!

Fortune's Embrace

In a tangled world, you might just find,
The silly moments that unwind.
With every fold, a comedy new,
Fortune's a friend, silly and true.

Beneath the folds where laughter lies,
Tripping on joy beneath the skies.
With every twist, a happy dance,
Embrace the luck, take a chance.

For fortune's tricks may make you grin,
While unraveling the messy din.
So wear your joy with a funny flair,
In the unforeseen, you'll find your care.

Wrapped in Whimsy

Around my neck, a twisty knot,
Colors bright, a cheerful spot.
With every breeze, it dances free,
A silly sight, oh what a spree!

Friends point and giggle, what a flair,
"Is it a fashion or a bear?"
I wink and laugh, they shake their heads,
In my joyful wraps, no dull threads!

Bobbing heads like wayward balloons,
Caught in the wind of silly tunes.
Each loop a jibe, each fringe a jest,
Who knew my flair would be the best?

So let them gawk, let laughter bloom,
In playful folly, flavors zoom.
Embrace the wild, turn humor high,
In whimsy's warmth, the heart can fly.

Happenstance in Hues

A splash of red, a dash of blue,
Oh, what a sight, a vivid view!
Patterns clash, yet feel so right,
Like mismatched socks on a Saturday night.

I wear my joy in tangled threads,
While neighbors peek from cozy beds.
"What's that mess?" they squint and stare,
I call it art, they call it wear!

Shimmering shades all twist and twirl,
Each color sings, a vibrant whirl.
In unexpected styles, giggles find,
Conundrums perk while life unwinds.

With every fold, the chaos spins,
Unexpected fun, where laughter begins.
So join the dance, let hues collide,
In messy jests, let hearts abide!

Against the Chill of Routine

Oh daily grind, your chill's so stark,
I drape myself in rainbow spark.
A cozy wrap against the dull,
Who knew that warmth could come with lull?

Each loop a wink to break the bleak,
I strut my stuff, hear laughter peak.
While coffee brews in somber mugs,
My flair ignites with playful shrugs.

A giggle slips, a chuckle roars,
As I make faces, coffee pours.
Routine may call, but I resist,
With silly flair on every twist!

So here's to joy, with every thread,
In colors bright, let worries shed.
For in this warmth, I take my stand,
A rebel's cheer, the joy unplanned.

The Gradient of Joy

From pastel shades to neon bright,
A gradient of fun takes flight.
Each layer wrapped, a snappy tease,
With every twist, I aim to please.

A mishmash of hues, they all collide,
In riotous laughter, I take pride.
I strut down streets, a jester's glee,
What's that? A pop of polka dot me!

When winter chills, I throw on flair,
Fashion faux pas? I do not care!
Each hue a grin, each thread a grin,
In this joyful riot, let fun begin!

So bring the colors, bring the cheer,
In vibrant plays, we persevere.
For life's a canvas, bright and free,
In playful strokes, it's you and me!

Knots of Fortune in Color

Tangled threads in vibrant cheer,
A slipknot's fate, oh so near.
Twists and turns, a jolly mess,
Every pull brings new success.

Laughter loops in every hue,
Winding paths, a silly view.
Colors clash, but hearts align,
In this game of chance, we shine.

The more we twist, the more we play,
Unexpected joys come out to stay.
With each knot, a story grows,
Whimsy blooms wherever it goes.

In tangled joy, we find our way,
Knot by knot, we laugh and sway.
Each color wraps us up, you see,
In this funny dance of glee.

The Charm of the Unplanned Wrap

A sudden gust and off it flies,
Looping 'round like a surprise.
A cloak of wind, it makes us grin,
Unruly fun, let the day begin!

Each toss and flail, a chance to play,
Chasing dreams that swirl away.
Wavy lines hold stories tight,
While laughter dances in the light.

Unexpected hugs from fabric bright,
Wrapping us up, oh what a sight!
Carefree twists embrace the air,
Life's little joys are everywhere.

With each unplanned embrace and flap,
We find the charm in fate's mishap.
So let it whirl, let it sway,
In the chaos, we find our way.

Soft Threads of Happening

Gentle fibers are drawn to play,
Whimsical dances lead the way.
Threads unite in playful schemes,
Crafting laughter from our dreams.

A twisting game of hide and seek,
Soft whispers make our spirits peak.
Each connection, a giggle shared,
In the woven joy, we are spared.

Serendipity's warm embrace,
In every fold, a smiling face.
Colors blend, and stories bloom,
In every twist, we find our room.

From selfies tangled in delight,
To humorous chats that spark the night.
Threads of life, both bright and fun,
In this soft world, we are one.

A Tapestry of Joyful Surprises

Each thread a tale, a chuckle spun,
In playful fibers, laughter's begun.
Surprises tucked in every seam,
Fueling our wild, whimsical dream.

A colorful dash around the bend,
Unexpected fun that never ends.
Patterns shifting, bold and bright,
In the merry dance of day and night.

Tangles that tickle, knots that tease,
In this fabric-fueled life, we seize.
Crafted moments in joyful hues,
Every twist brings playful news.

In a world where looms do play,
We find the funny in the fray.
With hearty laughs and shared delight,
We weave our lives, both day and night.

The Quiet Magic of Twisted Fibers

A bundle of threads, oh what a sight,
Spinning tales of laughter, day and night.
Colors collide in a whimsical dance,
Each twist whispers secrets, fate's little chance.

With yarn in hand and a grin so wide,
Knots of mischief, nothing to hide.
Patterns emerge that tickle the brain,
Each loop a joke, each stitch a gain.

In the basket of chaos, joy hides well,
Waiting for moments we can't quite tell.
Twisted together, our worries unwind,
Laughter unfolds, leaving woes behind.

So, embrace the fibers, let your heart roam,
In this funny yarn, we all find home.

Hidden Beauty in Stitched Adventures

In a pocket of threads, a story's unfurled,
Each stitch is a giggle, in colors swirled.
From tangled beginnings to straightened ends,
Crafting a journey with odd little bends.

Laughter erupts with every small miss,
Where patterns confuse, sweet chaos exists.
Every knot a moment of serendipitous cheer,
A whirl of fabric where friends draw near.

With needles as wands and yarn as our plight,
We weave our adventures in the soft moonlight.
Every pull and tug brings a story anew,
A delightful tapestry woven just for you.

Lace through the laughter, let joy lead our way,
In this stitched-up world, forever we'll play.

A Soft Embrace of Fate

Under a pile of fuzzy delight,
Life's little quirks bring such a bite.
Every soft hug hides a wink or two,
Fate plays its hand in the silliest cue.

Twisted together, we can't help but grin,
Wayward stitches where stories begin.
Each loop holds a giggle, each fringe a laugh,
Life's funny game is a cozy craft.

From lumps to loops and bends in between,
Fate's furry fabric is our routine.
Knit with chuckles, we adapt and sway,
Embracing fluff that brightens our day.

So when yarn spills over in a funny way,
Just laugh it off—it's a grand display.

Harmony in Knotted Dreams

In the dance of twirls, our dreams take flight,
With purling mishaps that feel just right.
Knots of silliness, woven in glee,
Each twist a chuckle, much like the sea.

Tangles and twirls, we knot up our fates,
Where whimsy and warmth open all the gates.
Each tug on the thread unravels a tale,
Of laughter and joy—let our spirits sail.

In the land of loops where absurdity flows,
Knotted up moments are how laughter grows.
Together we weave a fabric of dreams,
Where funny adventures burst at the seams.

So join in the fun and grab your own yarn,
In this jolly embrace we all feel the charm.

Stitched Together by Luck

One sunny day, a hat fell down,
It landed right on a cat's frown.
The cat wore it proud, quite a sight,
Turning heads with pure delight.

A sock flew past in a gusty breeze,
Danced with a squirrel, it did as it pleased.
They twirled around like a merry pair,
No wardrobe was safe, all clothes laid bare.

A mitten waved to a wayward glove,
They jived and twirled, just like a dove.
The dance was wild, the laughter loud,
In a world where chaos felt so proud.

When evening came, the moon did glow,
Each mismatched piece revealed its show.
With stitches coarse but tales so grand,
A fabric of fortune, unplanned and spanned.

Patterns of the Heart

In a market filled with vibrant hues,
A scarf was snatched by a pair of shoes.
They twirled and twinkled, causing a scene,
As tacos laughed, it was all quite keen.

A button popped, ricocheted in glee,
Leading a dance between two cups of tea.
They spilled their secrets, giggling away,
In patterns of chance, they chose to play.

A belt found a shoe, a bet they made,
To leap and laugh in a grand charade.
Missed a dance move, fell in a heap,
Unraveled in joy, not a soul could peep.

At the end of the day, all came to rest,
A wacky collection, each one the best.
Stitched together from laughter and cheer,
In a fabric of friendship, they'd shed every fear.

The Breeze of Fortuitous Moments

A windy day on a slender street,
A cap was chasing some fast-moving feet.
It caught a ride on a dog's wagging tail,
Causing a ruckus, a wild, funny trail.

A cloth napkin started to sway,
Caught in the wind, it just wanted to play.
It danced with a feather, a sight to behold,
In a circus of chaos, their stories unfolded.

A clumsy scarf slipped from a knotted tie,
Landed on a bicycle rolling by.
The rider then giggled; her hair went askew,
While the bike pedals sang a tune so blue.

As the sun set low, the tales piled high,
A patchwork of laughter kissed the sky.
With each twist and turn, fate took its shot,
Creating tomorrows from joyous knots.

Yarn of Chance

Once in a park, a yarn ball rolled,
It tangled a poodle, brave and bold.
With tails entwined, they raced in glee,
Creating a scene that was pure comedy.

Two gloves decided they'd take a chance,
In a silly, sparkly, moonlit dance.
Their fingers met in a jolly embrace,
Spinning wildly, no need for grace.

A thread unspooled, found a quirky mate,
Joined hands with a sock to share their fate.
They plotted and schemed to knit a grand plan,
To catch the giggles from every young fan.

Under the stars, they spun tales anew,
Of yarns and wonders, and laughter too.
In a tapestry woven with joy and flight,
Every twist and turn felt just so right.

A Tapestry of Unexpected Meetings

In a café, a stray thread flows,
A hat too big and a sock that glows.
They share a giggle, spill their drinks,
Twists of fate, oh how it stinks!

Lattes swirl, a dance in foam,
With mismatched boots, they claim their home.
A wink and nod, a laugh that's loud,
Two silly souls, they gather a crowd!

Out in the park, a kite goes high,
With tangled strings, they touch the sky.
A dance with squirrels, a jogger's glare,
Who knew chaos could lead to flair?

As sunset glows, they share a grin,
The wildest tales where laughs begin.
A tapestry woven, threads in play,
Celebrate mishaps in a quirky way.

Threads of Fate Unraveled

A button popped on a silly coat,
He trips and lands on a floating boat.
She laughs so hard, the water splashes,
While ducks quack loudly, the moment crashes!

In the mix of yarns, colors collide,
A knitting club where puns reside.
One crafts a sweater the size of a whale,
Each stitch a giggle, a comical tale!

Lost in the rows of tangled knits,
They find joy in mismatched hits.
A clap of thunder, a sudden rain,
Their laughter echoes, despite the pain!

As night falls down, stories unfold,
Each thread a journey, each laugh a gold.
Together they weave a humor spree.
In threads of fate, they dance carefree.

Cozy Twists of Destiny

At a yard sale, one quirky find,
A llama mug with a smile unlined.
They trade tall tales with quips in between,
Who knew a cup could stir up such a scene?

Eating ice cream, it drips and flows,
A race to catch it, a laughter explodes.
She slips on sprinkles, he shuts his eyes,
In a world of dairy, serendipity lies!

A midnight stroll, a dance with a broom,
They spin and twirl, causing a zoom.
Neighbors peek out, faces aglow,
Who knew mischief could steal the show?

With each twist, the evening grows bright,
In cozy chaos, they find sheer delight.
Together they tread, humor their guide,
In a tapestry stitched with joy side by side.

The Fabric of Serendipity

In a thrift shop, with treasures galore,
They find a mix of laughs to explore.
A tuxedo cat in a bow tie snug,
Who knew thrift could spark such a hug?

A dance-off starts with a quirky twist,
Two mismatched socks both clench their fists.
The floor's a stage, the tunes they steal,
With each silly move, they seal the deal!

Late-night debates on sprinkles versus nuts,
They bicker on toppings, through all of the cuts.
When ice cream falls, a mess is found,
But giggles echo, love's background sound!

These moments woven, a fabric true,
Of joy and laughter, with love in the brew.
A patchwork life, with each little mess,
Is a tribute to laughter, a comic success.

Echoes of Colorful Encounters

In the market, vibrant threads sway,
A lady dropped a bright green array.
I tripped over, took a tumble,
Now our laughter's a joyful rumble.

Each hue an echo of chance's call,
Twisting and turning, we dance with them all.
Colors weave tales of the day we met,
A tapestry of laughter, you won't forget.

Spilled tea on the fabric, oh what a mess!
But your smile says it's just silliness.
We share a glance, both start to grin,
Two vibrant souls, let the fun begin!

In threads of orange and ocean blue,
Every twist leads to something new.
Amidst the chaos, our hearts collide,
In the whimsy of colors, we take a ride.

The Charm of Unplanned Paths

Stumbling down the street, I spied a hat,
Off it went, rolling like a playful cat.
Chasing it down, we both start to race,
Bumping into strangers, a colorful embrace.

A picnic at dusk with jam and bread,
Who knew the path would lead to this thread?
We laughed so hard, found mustard stains,
Moments like these fill our silly brains.

Twisting our scarves, we dance in the park,
Under the glow of the evening's spark.
With every turn, we form new tales,
Meandering paths where nothing fails.

Every mishap a story to unfold,
Like mismatched socks, we're bravely bold.
Let's embrace the charm in paths unplanned,
Together we'll wander, a silly band.

Weaving Whispers

In a cafe bustling with all the buzz,
Our drinks collide with a hilarious fuzz.
You spilled your mocha, I coughed on my tea,
Mixing flavors made quite the glee!

The barista compared us to a yarn ball,
Sipping and laughing, we had a ball.
With each whispered secret, our tales entwined,
In the fabric of friendship, two hearts aligned.

We tossed napkins like late-night confetti,
Trying to catch crumbs, our move was quite Betty.
With each sip, we wove a new joke,
Laughter delicious, like homemade smoke!

Stitching together these moments of cheer,
Who knew that whispers could draw us near?
Like threads of joy, they blend and unite,
In the tapestry of giggles, our hearts ignite.

Colors that Connect

At the paint shop, hues in a row,
You picked bright pink, I chose the glow.
Who knew our choices would ignite a chat,
About wild socks and a dancing cat?

Sliding through aisles with brushes in hand,
We painted the walls, oh what a stand!
With every stroke, connections grew wide,
In splashes of laughter, we took the ride.

Mismatched palettes, a colorful sight,
Your vibrant green, my fiery bright.
We pranced like peacocks, all swirls and twirls,
Our paint-splattered clothes adorned like pearls!

With each turn of the brush, we felt that spark,
Colors that connect, lighting the dark.
In the mess of shades, friendships bloom,
Through paint and laughter, we face the room.

Charmed Threads of Destiny

In a corner shop, I found a hue,
Bright pink and blue, it sang anew.
Wrapped it around, I felt like a star,
My friends just laughed, 'How bizarre!'

Twisted and turned in fabric delight,
A fashion show, oh what a sight!
The cat joined in, with patterned glee,
You'd think it was a runway spree!

With every loop, I spun a tale,
Of colors dancing, never pale.
It slipped and slid, oh what a chase,
The floor became my art-filled space.

So here's to loops that twist and twine,
With every swirl, we feel divine.
Each fabric caught a giggle or two,
In the charm of threads, we all just grew.

A Dance of Colors in the Breeze

A bright red twist laughed in the wind,
It danced around as if it sinned.
Each color pirouetted with grace,
In this funny, vibrant race.

Green caught blue in a playful hug,
Spinning about, they were quite snug.
With every flutter, our spirits soared,
Who knew such joy life could afford?

A yellow patch joined for a laugh,
Crimson teased with a silly half.
Together they jived, a comical crew,
Just fabric and fate—oh, who knew?

So when you see a sashay or twirl,
Remember the dance, let colors unfurl.
For every twist tells tales anew,
In the lightness of fabric, dreams come true.

The Embrace of Sunlit Fabrics

Once draped in cotton, I found a friend,
A tangle of threads that had no end.
It wrapped me tight, with a cheeky grin,
We laughed so hard, where to begin?

The sun beamed bright, gold yarns did shine,
As I twirled around, feeling divine.
But a gust of wind sent me astray,
My hat took off—oh what a display!

In shadows we played, in sunshine we gleamed,
A patchwork of laughter, all brightly schemed.
With every toss and every jibe,
The fabric spun tales of joy and vibe.

As night descends, whispers of dreams,
With swirls of joy and soft, giggly beams.
In this colorful hug, we grew more light,
In the embrace of brightness, all feels right.

Intricate Paths of Warmth and Wonder

Each thread weaves stories of silly delight,
With patterns that giggle in the soft light.
A twist here, a knot there, playful and bold,
In the fabric of life, such wonders unfold.

Bright plaids and polka dots danced in the sun,
Every fiber inviting us just to have fun.
But one fateful loop turned into a mess,
As I tripped on fashion—what a hot dress!

The threads tangled up in comical flair,
A wrap became a snare, oh, beware!
Yet laughter erupted in our tangled plight,
As we rolled on the floor, oh what a sight!

So let's tread these paths with a wink and a grin,
For in each entanglement, joy will begin.
With warmth woven deep in every embrace,
In the tapestry of life, we all find our place.

Threads in the Wind

A snooze on a bench, a breeze so bold,
A hat flew by, what a sight to behold.
An errant scarf caught on a passing shoe,
I chased it down, who knew what it'd do?

With colors bright, some stripes, some dots,
It wrapped my face like a pirate's plot.
A wave ensued, laughter filled the air,
While fashion critics just stopped to stare.

I twirled and danced, avoiding the trees,
As onlookers chuckled, and I said, "Please!"
In jest, I waved, the fun had just begun,
In this wild chase, who could not have fun?

When threads become friends in quirky play,
Life's little quirks lead us astray.
For joy is found in the silliest spins,
In a world so bright, where the laughter begins.

The Unexpected Weave

A yarn shop's delight on a Tuesday morn,
I ventured inside, ever so worn.
Bobbins and spools, they danced in delight,
Until one rolled away, a comical sight.

It hit an old lady, who stood by the door,
"I wasn't expecting that!" she did roar.
We both burst out laughing, itchy with glee,
Who knew yarn could bring such hilarity?

Strands tangled together, like stories untold,
In this crafty corner, we laughed when bold.
As fabric raced by, like a runaway train,
We schemed and we plotted, driving off the mundane.

In patterns so random, we spun our own fate,
With giggles and stitches, we'd navigate.
Each color a chuckle, each fiber a cheer,
Together, we wove a tapestry here.

An Intertwined Journey

Two friends on the road, both clumsy and spry,
Wore mismatched knits as we waved to the sky.
A gust of wind picked up our attire,
And whisked us along, ever higher and higher.

One scarf got caught on a passing truck's grill,
It flapped like a flag, a sight to fulfill.
We giggled and struggled, trying to win,
Chasing fashion while losing our skin!

With loops and knots, we formed a new kin,
From tangled threads, our laughter wore thin.
At every odd corner, a twist or a turn,
Life tossed us about—oh, there's so much to learn!

But in every misstep, a dance would arise,
With twirls in our walks, and bright, gleeful sighs.
We spun through the chaos, embraced the disarray,
In every faux pas, we found joy on the way.

Beneath the Cloth of Life

In closets of chaos, fabrics reside,
A quilt of memories, where secrets abide.
Some socks are unmatched, and sweaters are torn,
Yet each stitch recalls the moments we've worn.

We draped 'round our shoulders, bold patterns and hues,
Then tripped on the fringe, while sharing our news.
The fabric of friendship, so tangled yet snug,
We laughed till we cried, like a well-stitched rug.

A patchwork of stories, in colors so bright,
In laughter, we tangled, from morning 'til night.
A sudden breeze caught a curtain with flair,
It whipped through the room, with fun in the air.

As dust bunnies joined us in this playful review,
We twirled through the fabric, as best friends do.
In the weave of our lives, let the laughter entwine,
For each quirk and mishap is truly divine.

Unraveled Dreams on a Breezy Day

A twist of fate, the wind does play,
My thoughts take flight, they run away.
A tangles here, a knot up there,
Oh, how I wish I'd seen the air!

With laughter spilling from my lips,
I chase the dance of fabric's flips.
Each gust a cheeky little wink,
In this mad game, I start to think!

Colors swirl, a playful fight,
They tease the day, from dawn to night.
Like socks that wander, hide and seek,
I find new joys in mischief's peak!

In every twist, a giggle springs,
Life's silly threads create such things.
So come, embrace the breezy play,
And laugh with dreams that fly away!

Life's Fabric: Woven Moments

In stitches fine and patterns bold,
Life weaves its stories, bright and old.
A quirky patch upon my chest,
Reminds me I'm not like the rest!

Thread the needle, make a joke,
Each slip a chance, each snag a poke.
The tapestry of time unfolds,
With every laugh, new tales it holds!

A speck of paint upon my shoe,
A mark of fun and something new.
In every corner, joy to find,
The fabric of life is mostly blind!

So grab a piece, let's stitch together,
Through all the storms, no matter the weather.
With whims of fate and endless thread,
We'll weave our laughter, never dread!

A Journey in Every Loop

Round and round, the yarn does spin,
A journey starts when we begin.
With every loop a giggly chance,
To dance through life, to twirl, to prance!

A slip, a slide, oh what a mess,
Yet here I am, in full success!
Unraveling tales from my own hand,
With each odd twist, I make my stand.

So off we go, into the fray,
No map in sight, we're led astray.
Yet in the chaos, there's always cheer,
As loops and curls bring friends near!

With every turn, a laugh awaits,
Life's tapestry, it's never late.
So grab your thread, let's weave anew,
In every twist, let joy ensue!

Threads of Comfort and Serendipity

A tangle here, a cuddle there,
Threads of fortune fill the air.
With every snag, a laugh breaks free.
Life's tiny mishaps are key, you see!

Wrap me close in colors bright,
A cozy hug, pure delight.
Laughter blooms in every seam,
Life's fabric crafted from a dream!

When things go wrong, I simply sigh,
For in that moment, I learn to fly.
With each soft loop, a story grows,
Blissful threads shooting through my toes!

In every twist, a smile I find,
With playful knots that fate designed.
So here's to joy in every thread,
Where laughter lives and worries shed!

The Fabric of Fortuity

In the closet, colors collide,
A rainbow in a tangled slide.
Hats and gloves, all play their part,
Yet the socks just roll their eyes and dart.

With a twist and a turn, we all laugh,
A knit and a purl, our fancy craft.
Worn in styles, quite out of place,
Each slip a giggle, each loop a grace.

Friends gather round, to sip and weave,
The tales that grew from what we believe.
With every flutter, a new buffoon,
Who knew misfits could dance under the moon?

So raise a glass to fate's wild thread,
To patterns stitched where once we tread.
Laughter and joy, our fabric's delight,
In every misadventure, we take flight!

Beneath the Whispering Veil

A curtain sways, with secrets to tell,
Whispers of fabric, dancing so well.
Trying to style a look all my own,
End up a jester, in clothes overblown.

A tangled scarf goes flying amok,
Caught on a doorknob, what a fine luck!
The cat takes a leap, paws fly through the air,
Knocked down some cushions, oh, what a scare!

In a world of folds, and colors so bright,
Each mishap just makes the evening feel right.
From tangled yarn to frayed edges bold,
We laugh at our stories, and let them unfold.

Laughter erupts at the silliest sights,
Fate's silly dress-up, our greatest delights.
So drape on a giggle, let fashion be free,
For what is a style, but fun times with glee?

Misty Mornings and Twisted Threads

Misty morn, with threads of confusion,
Can't find my way through this fabric illusion.
Lost in the weaves of yesterday's style,
With each twist and turn, I trip for a mile.

Pulling out colors, oh, what a sight,
A polka dot vest? It can't be just right!
Each piece I choose turns a neighbor's flat,
They point and they laugh at this outfit's chat.

Yet joy blossoms, with each thread we stitch,
Tagging along, like a dog that won't quit!
Our fashion parade turns into a race,
Who'll win the prize for the best-dressed face?

So let's spin our stories, and make them real,
Each knot and each knot, it's all part of the deal.
Amid misty mornings, let laughter convect,
For what is a day but a chance to connect?

When Stitches Meet Fate

A needle's dance, oh, what a disaster,
In my hands, the thread pulls faster!
Each tug gives me hope that it won't all break,
Yet fashion mishaps are fate's funny wake.

Stitch and twist, a picturesque mess,
My friends all declare it's a style to impress!
But the sweater I made, it's crooked and sheer,
A loser's delight, yet I hold it so dear.

Here comes a buddy, with laughter to share,
He wore the same thing, in a different pair!
Two fashion faux pas, side by side,
In this quirky world, let's laugh and collide.

So when those stitches bring smiles from fate,
We'll cherish these moments, never too late.
For in every slip, and each tangled thread,
There lies a great joy, where laughter is bred.

Embracing the Threads of Time

In a jumble of colors, I found a surprise,
A knot in my pocket, a twist of the skies.
Laughter erupted, it stole my good sense,
Fashion's a puzzle, with laughs to dispense.

A swirl of a fiber, a wacky delight,
My neighbor's cat sneezed, oh what a sight!
With needles a-chatter, we knitted in glee,
Each stitch was a joke, just you wait and see.

A hat on a chair, it leaped off the hook,
With each little twist, we wrote our own book.
Who knew that these threads could dance and could prance,
In the world of the wacky, we took a mad chance.

So here's to the fibers, the frolicsome thread,
To giggles and stitches that bounce in your head.
With laughter as glue, we tangle and twine,
Embracing the chaos, it's truly divine.

Weavings of a Whimsical Destiny

Woven through laughter, a tale took its flight,
A ball of bright yarn rolled into the night.
It danced on the table, it jived with the cat,
As I chased down the threads, tripped over the mat.

A closet of wonders, where mishaps abound,
A rogue sock was sitting, oh what a clown!
With each little stitch, craziness brewed,
Who knew yarn could lead to such moods?

Around the corner, my buddy would grin,
Embarking on adventures that made our heads spin.
With a twist and a laugh, we created our fate,
Each loop a reminder: it's never too late.

So gather your fibers, your frisky old crew,
In this knitting cabaret, there's fun just for you.
With joy in the stitches, our fibers we'll share,
Weaving up stories, beyond compare.

Spirals of Joy and Unexpected Knits

In a curl of a yarn, joy started to spin,
Looped around moments, where laughter begins.
With each little twist, more fun's on the way,
The yarn climbed a ladder, and brought out the play.

There's a cat on my lap, who's tangled in thread,
As I try to knit, he's plotting instead.
With a paw and a pounce, he leaps with such cheer,
Transforming my project into a circus, oh dear!

Forget all the patterns, the rules of the art,
Just follow the giggles that burst from the heart.
In spirals of mayhem, our stitches entwine,
Creating a fabric where humor will shine.

So let's break the norms, with wild expectation,
In the world of the quirky, there's no limitation.
With each little knot, we'll summon a grin,
Spirals of laughter, let the fun begin!

Joyous Yarns in Life's Serendipity

From a basket of yarns, bright colors do flow,
Each twist and each turn brings a chuckle, you know.
A squirrel with my scarf?! What a sight to behold,
I chased after giggles, as chaos unfolds.

Lost in the fabric, the patterns collide,
With needles a-tapping, our laughter's the guide.
We knit up our stories, while tea's on the boil,
With every good snicker, we savor the toil.

A dribble of tea spills on the floor in a dance,
As I swerve to catch joy and not miss my chance.
In yarns of the silly, our world becomes bright,
We'll twirl in the warmth, wrapped up and light.

So here's to the moments, so quirky and grand,
To stitches and stories that go hand in hand.
With joyous creations and friendships so true,
In this carnival of yarns, there's enough room for you!

The Mystique of Fortuitous Knits

In a shop filled with colors so bright,
I stumbled on yarn, what a silly sight!
My fingers got tangled, oh what a mess,
Yet laughter erupted, it turned to success.

A pattern I chose, no clue what it meant,
Blindfolded crafting, my time was well spent.
With stitches so crooked, I wore it with pride,
A garment of giggles, my joyful guide.

Then came a cat, all fluffy and round,
Deciding my project was fine for a crown.
With a leaping grace, it jumped right on me,
And now I'm the queen of absurdity!

But in every mishap, there's laughter to gain,
Knots in my yarn only drive me insane.
Fortune's a jester, it keeps me in cheer,
With each silly twist, the bliss becomes clear.

Soft Embraces and Sudden Joys

A cozy cocoon, I dive into hues,
Soft threads entwine, oh what joyous news!
In the attic, I found a forgotten treasure,
A patchwork of wit, stitched with pleasure.

Around me they dance, those whimsical threads,
Creating odd patterns where nonsense treads.
A sweater that wobbles, a hat shaped like cheese,
Each piece tells a story and tickles with ease.

The dog joins the fun, with yarn in a flurry,
Rolling and tumbling, oh what a hurry!
He thinks it's a game, this playful affair,
With every misstep, it's joy in the air.

So here's to the laughter that stitches us tight,
In whims of creation, we find pure delight.
Each twist of the yarn brings wonders anew,
Making hearts knit closer, with much to pursue.

A Bind of Yarns in Gratefulness

A spool of colors, oh what a spree,
Came softly unwinding, giggling with glee.
I tried to be crafty, failed yet again,
But laughter is magic, it conquers the pain.

A knitting crusade, with needles so bright,
Each loop was a battle, a whimsical fight.
The cat thought my yarn was a game to explore,
Chasing those threads, it brought joy by the score.

Caught in a tangle, I stumbled and spun,
My creation transformed into a quirky bun.
With a wink and a nudge, I wore it with flair,
Life's little hiccups bring joy in the air!

So here's to the binds of silly delight,
When things go awry, and laughter takes flight.
In the chaos of yarn, we find joy untold,
Each stitch full of giggles, dreams bright and bold.

Enigmatic Wraps of Delight

In winter's chill, a bundle tight,
A twist of color, oh what a sight!
Each layer snug, a hug from afar,
I'm wrapped in warmth, my style bizarre.

A flurry of fabric, a dance on the breeze,
Caught in a moment, oh how it teases!
I trip on patterns, my feet in a knot,
Who knew such tangles could bring me such plot?

The world's a stage, and here comes my flair,
With scarves that flutter, I strut with a stare!
What's that? A squirrel? In my fringe, it shows,
I chuckle and giggle, wherever I goes!

So cheers to the wraps that wrap us so tight,
And to the joy that makes us feel light!
In threads of laughter, we fashion our fate,
With whimsical whims, let's twirl before late.

A Tangle of Threads and Triumphs

A ball of yarn rolls under the bed,
Like tangled thoughts inside my head;
I pull and tug, the mess will unwind,
In laughter and chaos, I'm sweetly aligned.

My fingers dance, they hop and they skip,
Crafting a mess on a whimsical trip;
Each stitch a story, each knot a jest,
Who knew that fabric could bring such zest?

The neighbors peek from behind their blinds,
As I try to model these wonky designs;
With patterns of chaos, I prance and I twirl,
My clothes are an adventure, a topsy-turvy swirl!

So here's to the snags and the awkward attire,
With threads of delight that never expire!
In stitches and giggles, we weave through the day,
And celebrate life in our quirky ballet.

The Cloak of Serendipitous Moments

In a corner shop with a view to behold,
I spotted a find, a treasure untold;
A cloak of mischief, with colors so bright,
While giggling, I draped it and felt such delight!

Each flap a giggle, each fold a surprise,
Wrapped in a riddle that tickles the skies;
I spin like a whirlwind, not caring a bit,
For life's just a game, and I'm enwrapped in wit!

A misplaced turn leads to laughter and fun,
As I trip on my hem, but oh, what a run!
With every awkward moment, the joy leaps and bounds,
A saga of laughter, where upside-downs astound!

So here's to the cloak that carries us through,
With whimsical tales stitched in every hue;
In happenstance, we find our way to play,
With a chuckle and shimmy, we frolic each day!

Patterns of Love in Knitted Dreams

In the warmth of the yarn shop, I sit in a daze,
Fern green and crimson, oh what a maze!
As I knit and I purl, I dream of delight,
With patterns of love that shimmer and bite.

The needles clatter like hearts in a race,
Whispers of joy in this cozy space;
I drop a stitch, but it's laughter I taste,
With every new pattern, no moment's a waste!

My cat sees my yarn as a twinkling chase,
Pouncing on piles, what a curious face!
Oops, there goes that project, all frayed and torn,
A masterpiece born from the chaos, so worn!

So let's raise a toast to our crafted mistakes,
In every small tangle, a love story wakes;
With fibers of laughter stitched into our seams,
We knit our adventures in colorful dreams.

The Unexpected Pattern of Life

In a tangle of threads, I find my way,
Laughter dances, bright as the day.
Colors clash and twirl in my gaze,
Life's quirky chime keeps me amazed.

A knot here, a twist, the fabric sings,
Every stitch a surprise that joy brings.
Patches of antics sewn with delight,
A patchwork of fortune, oh what a sight!

Bumps and loops make a grand debut,
Every mishap yields something new.
In life's tapestry, each thread will play,
A wobbly weave brightens my day.

With a flick and a flap, I prance and sway,
Finding giggles in a quirky array.
Embracing the chaos as friends close in,
This whimsical fabric is where I begin.

Cozy Wraps and Joyful Discoveries

Wrapped in layers of vibrant glee,
I trip over joy like it's hiding in me.
A twist of humor that warms the soul,
Life's gentle embrace makes me feel whole.

Unexpected warmth in a chilly breeze,
I tumble and giggle, do as I please.
In bright patches of laughter, I roam,
Finding delight in the joys of home.

The fabric of friendship is snug and tight,
We laugh at the chaos, oh what a sight!
In wild patterns, our stories grow,
Each silly mishap, a splendid show.

Colors collide, a playful embrace,
Creating a memory, a wondrous trace.
With each wacky twirl, I'm lost in the spin,
Wrapped up in life, let the fun begin!

Weaving Through Life with Warmth

In shawls of laughter, we stroll along,
Life's silly dance, a delightful song.
Yarns of joy twist in whimsical ways,
Creating new tales for our bright days.

With each cozy twist, we share a grin,
As laughter echoes, the fun begins.
Threading the needle of joy, we play,
A tapestry of friendship lights the way.

In every loop, a story unfolds,
With kernels of humor in clothes of gold.
I weave through mishaps, the fabric smiles,
Embracing the goofy and running wild.

Clad in warmth, we embrace the surprise,
Life's quirky patchwork—oh how it ties!
With warmth and giggles, we navigate,
This ridiculous weave is truly great.

Colors That Whisper of the Unknown

In hues of chaos, secrets beckon me,
I follow the whispers that giggle with glee.
Stripes that challenge and dots that tease,
Life's playful palette puts me at ease.

A splash of craziness on quiet days,
Bringing a chuckle, in unexpected ways.
Twisting through patterns, I lose my fear,
Every pop of color brings me near.

Bright fabric of magic unfolds in my sight,
Tickling my senses, it feels so right.
In the tapestry of joy, I dance and sway,
Colors of laughter, leading the way.

Mismatched and merry, I take a spin,
Life's riotous hues draw me in.
Wrapped in the wonder of the unknown,
Each whimsical stitch feels like home.